The Amazing Chase was inspired by a rescue dog named Chase. This book is dedicated to him and to everyone who rescues, fosters, or adopts animals in need.

A very special thank you to my wife, Tresa. This book would not have been possible without her support. Her love of dogs and her passion for rescue is truly inspiring!

www.mascotbooks.com

The Amazing Chase

©2018 Steve Wize. All Rights Reserved. No part of this publication may be reproduced, stored in a retrieval system or transmitted in any form by any means electronic, mechanical, or photocopying, recording or otherwise without the permission of the author.

For more information, please contact:
Mascot Books
620 Herndon Parkway #320
Herndon, VA 20170
info@mascotbooks.com

Library of Congress Control Number: 2018900625

CPSIA Code: PBANG0518A
ISBN-13: 978-1-68401-781-2

Printed in the United States

DEAR PARENTS,

According to the ASPCA, 670,000 shelter dogs are put down each year in the United States. I hope that this book will inspire more individuals and families to adopt, not shop.

I hope too that as you share this book with your child, you use your time together to talk about the values that we can learn from our furry friends. Yes, dogs are cute and cuddly, but they also demonstrate many qualities and values that we want our children to have as well.

Like Chase, we all learn values throughout the journey of our lives. Dogs are brave, caring, fun, patient, eager, loyal, and loving. What great life lessons and values we can impart to our children by these examples. Take time as you share the book together to discuss these values, and remember that these are the things that make us a family.

Give your kids (and your dog) a hug tonight. Thank you for supporting dogs in need.

Sincerely,

STEVE

CUTE

Can we keep him?

In a perfect world,
every dog would have a

CUDDLY

BRAVE

Don't be scared, Chase.
You can do it!

LEARNING

Chase, stay!

CARING

FAST

Go get it, Chase!

EAGER

Good boy, Chase.

SLEEPY

Good night, Chase.

AMAZING FACTS ABOUT DOGS

- A dog's nose is unique like a person's fingerprint

- Dogs have 42 teeth

- A dog's sense of smell is 1,000 times stronger than a human's

- A dog's hearing is four times better than ours

- People have had dogs for pets for over 12,000 years. There are even paintings made by cave men in Spain of dogs

- There are 400 million dogs in the world

- The first animal to go into space was a dog

- The fastest dog on earth can run up to 45 mph

- Dogs can run as fast in the snow (27 mph) as the fastest human, Usain Bolt, can on land

- Dogs can't eat raisins, grapes, onions, chocolate, or garlic, or they get sick

- Dogs see better at night than humans

- Dogs are used to track down criminals (bad guys)

- Dogs can help with hunting, farmwork, security, and assisting those with disabilities, such as the blind

- Dogs dream just like people

- Dogs are descendants of wolves. That means the great-great-great-grandparent of your dog was actually a wolf!

- In the United States, a dog is adopted once every twenty seconds

- Approximately 1.6 million dogs are adopted each year

ABOUT US

One Big Happy Family

(Left to Right)
Butters (Black and White Shih Tzu) The Silly One
Ella (Black and White Pomeranian) The Sweet One
Sasha (White, Tan, and Black Pomeranian) The Smiley One
Sierra (White Shih Tzu) The Bossy One
Hamilton (Collie) The Kind One
Winston (Himalayan Cat) The Cuddly One

Steve Wize is a professional therapist at Mental Fitness, LLC in Cranberry Township, Pennsylvania. When he's not working, Steve enjoys hiking, disc golf, and walks with the family.

Steve and Tresa will be adding a new addition to the family with the birth of their first child in May of 2018.